YORK NOTES

General Editors: Professor A.N. Jeffares (*University of Stirling*) & Professor Suheil Bushrui (*American University of Beirut*)

Graham Greene

THE HEART OF THE MATTER

Notes by Mark Mortimer

BA (DUBLIN)
*Senior Lecturer, The British Institute in Paris,
Universities of London and Paris*

LONGMAN
YORK PRESS

YORK PRESS
Immeuble Esseily, Place Riad Solh, Beirut.

LONGMAN GROUP LIMITED
Longman House,
Burnt Mill,
Harlow,
Essex

First published 1985
ISBN 0 582 79241 X
Produced by Longman Group (FE) Ltd
Printed in Hong Kong

Contents

Part 1

Introduction

Family background and education

Graham Greene was born in 1904 into a well-to-do English upper middle-class family. He was thus a member of that section of English society to which he constantly harks back in his work, and to which many of his leading characters belong. He was educated at one of the less well-known public schools, Berkhamsted, where his father was headmaster, and where he seems to have acquired a lasting hatred for organised society. The English 'public school' of the time—an endowed secondary boarding school, preparing boys for the ancient universities or the public service—emphasised communal living, with its vast dormitories, semi-private lavatories and school 'crocodiles' (an organised file of pupils out for a walk), often an intolerable invasion of individual liberty for a sensitive person. Most of the author's future references to such institutions show hostility to their narrow morality, Victorian respectability, sense of 'fair play'. In *The Heart of the Matter*, for instance, Wilson and Fraser's old school, Downham, is an object of mockery, with it peculiar jargon, its school magazine, its not altogether disinterested anxiety to keep in touch with former students. Clearly Graham Greene was unhappy at school, for he made several adolescent attempts to end his life there and had to be treated by a psychoanalyst after running away. These 'very unhappy memories' as he calls them in his first volume of autobiography, *A Sort of Life* (1971), were followed by an academically undistinguished career at Balliol College, Oxford, where he published a volume of verse and made some lasting friends. When he left Oxford he had made no definite plans to become a writer.

Reception into the Catholic Church

In 1926, at the age of twenty-two, Graham Greene was received into the Catholic Church. Some of his greatest novels – *The Power and the Glory, The Heart of the Matter, The End of the Affair*—are concerned with specifically Catholic problems, though he has always rejected the label of 'Catholic novelist' and been irritated by any attempt of the Church to claim him. *The Heart of the Matter*, in particular, shows his Catholicism to be highly unorthodox. Stressing his left-wing opinions,

George Orwell (1903–1950) described him as the 'first Catholic fellow-traveller' and it should be remembered that *The Power and the Glory* was at one time banned by the Vatican. At all events, his reasoned acceptance of the Catholic faith—after an unhappy adolescence and a troubled early manhood—appears to have given him the anchor of certainty he needed. He has never turned back.

Journalism and foreign travel

After some experiences of newspaper work in the provinces he worked successively for *The Times* (as sub-editor 1926–30) and for *The Spectator* (as film critic 1935–9 and, later, as literary editor 1940–1). Several assignments abroad confirmed his gifts as a journalist and enabled him to show his skill as a writer of travel books: *Journey without Maps* (Liberia), *The Lawless Roads* (Mexico). The latter was to provide him with much of the material for one of his greatest novels, *The Power and the Glory*, which won him the Hawthornden Prize for Literature in 1941 and established him as a writer to be reckoned with in modern fiction. Many of his other novels are set in foreign countries: *England made me* in Sweden, *Our Man in Havana* in Cuba, *The Quiet American* in Indochina, and *The Comedians* in Haiti. Everywhere his observant eye and impeccable style are used to reveal the world behind the façade, in its true political, economic or social colours. Whatever worlds are being depicted—Capitalist or Communist, Fascist or Colonialist—the message is much the same: beneath the veneer of so-called civilisation, decay and corruption, misery, lust and greed predominate. Man-made solutions are doomed to failure, for man's natural state is the jungle. Graham Greene's extensive travel, his well-trained eye and ear, his human sympathy and deep perception all lead him to confirm this view.

Influence of the cinema

His experience as film critic with *The Spectator* strengthened a boyhood enthusiasm for this fast-growing medium. He wrote the script for the films *The Third Man* and *Fallen Idol*, and many of his novels have been successfully filmed. The influence of the cinema, like that of the thriller, of detective fiction, of adventure stories, is pervasive, seen especially in his use of exotic settings, of brilliant 'shots', of a frequent exploitation of 'montage' (a film technique by which contrasting shots or sequences follow one another without interruption, in order to suggest a single idea or impression or mood). Essentially a man of his time, in his interest in outlaws and spies, gangsters and gunmen, Greene revels in danger and pursuit, crime and violence, horror and betrayal. It would be hard to find another writer who has demonstrated so effectively how the framework of the modern thriller and the technique of the modern cinema can be harnessed to the novel form, that is, the novel as conceived with a clear plot, living characters, excitement and suspense.

Achievement as a writer

Greene's achievement as a writer is considerable, his success unquestioned. One American writer has called him 'Britain's chief literary export', and his works have been translated into many foreign languages. Apart from twenty-five novels and three volumes of short stories, he has published five plays, three travel books, many critical essays, poetry, books for children, biographies and two volumes of autobiography. The range and bulk of his work are staggering. Yet it is as a novelist that he will be best remembered, for it is chiefly as a novelist that he has borne witness to his time, which includes two great wars, the Great Depression, Fascist horrors and Colonialist cruelties, as well as the extraordinary strides made by the media and communications generally. Shaking off the inhibitions a respectable establishment background might have been expected to confer, he has continued, as one critic wrote, 'turning in his minority report'. No future social historian can afford to neglect his work. Eagerly employing those modern techniques already cited (cinema, press, thrillers, detective stories) he lays claim to a high place in the long line of English novelists, recalling Charles Dickens (1812–70) in his evocation of childhood; Joseph Conrad (1856–1924) and Robert Louis Stevenson (1850–94) in his ability to tell an exciting tale; and not neglecting the experimentalists—James Joyce (1882–1941), Virginia Woolf (1882–1941)—in his use of the interior monologue. Too rebellious and different to be considered a true-blue Englishman (expatriate, Catholic, left-wing); too popular to please the highbrows; and maybe too prolific to be deemed an exacting artist, he has always gone his own way, perfecting his style, enlarging his horizons, following his conscience. *The Heart of the Matter* is a superb example of the novelist's craft; it is among his best works.

A note on the text

The Heart of the Matter was first published in Great Britain by William Heinemann, London, in 1948. A revised edition was published in 1971 by Heinemann and The Bodley Head, London, with an introduction by the author, which provides the student with valuable information: extracts from the random notes kept in Sierra Leone, and subsequently used in the story; remarks about the 'two very different novels' he had in mind; his later feelings about Scobie's religious scruples. In particular, we are told about the author's decision to make certain changes in the book, mainly the re-insertion of a chapter which was part of the original draft but had been left out of the earlier editions. 'Now I have re-inserted the passage so that this edition for the first time presents the novel as I first wrote it, apart from minor revisions, perhaps more numerous than in any other novel in this edition' (p.XIV, Heinemann 1971 edition). The revisions referred to are, notably, the omission of the sentence 'Away in the town the cocks began to crow for the false dawn' at the end of Book Two, Part I, Chapter 3, Section 2 and several mentions of the word 'Catholic'—all of which serve to lighten the stress on the religious side of the book.

The novel was first published in paperback by Penguin Books, Harmondsworth, in 1962 and reset and reprinted later from the Collected Edition of 1971. It was first published in the United States of America by The Viking Press, New York, in 1948; and the Viking Compass Revised Edition appeared in 1974.

Part 2

Summaries

of THE HEART OF THE MATTER

A general summary

The novel tells the story of a fifty-year-old Deputy Commissioner of Police in a West African British colony during the last world war. After fifteen years of service, this unromantic hero, Scobie, 'a dull middle-aged police officer who had failed for promotion' (Bk. Two, III, 1/3)* has come to love the people and the place, despite widespread corruption, unhealthy climate and pervasive sordidness. A convert to the Catholic Church, he is a practising Catholic with a genuine love of God and a natural, deep-seated goodness. Permanently saddened by the loss of his only child (a little girl of nine) some years earlier, he feels that his peaceful life in the colony is threatened by his relationship with his wife, for whom he feels pity rather than love, and whose happiness he is determined to protect at all costs. In order to send her on holiday to South Africa, he borrows money from Yusef, a Syrian of doubtful character, and gradually finds his integrity eroded, although he had always been the justest and most incorruptible of men. In the absence of his wife, and again motivated more by pity than by love, he has a affair with one of the survivors of a torpedoed ship who are brought to the colony, a young widow of nineteen whose husband is among the lost. When his wife returns, earlier than expected, he is thus caught between two women, neither of whom he wants to hurt; and his self-respect is impaired by the irregularities he feels bound to commit through compassion or necessity.

His situation is further complicated by the spying activities of Wilson, a secret agent sent out to keep an eye on the diamond smuggling (who falls in love with his wife); and his moral problems are heightened by his obligations as a Catholic. Through his fault, his faithful servant, Ali, is murdered; and seeing no other solution to his plight, he commits a carefully camouflaged suicide, which is unmasked as such after his death. While there are vivid descriptions of life in the colony and many striking thumbnail sketches, the main theme of the novel is Scobie's twofold dilemma: how to reconcile his feelings for two women and how to honour his Catholic beliefs. It is a tribute to the

---

* *For convenience, this style of reference will be adopted hereafter, thus indicating in this case Book Two, Part III, Chapter 1, Section 3.*

author's narrative skill that he invests this twofold dilemma with all the excitement of a modern thriller.

Detailed summaries

BOOK ONE, PART I

Chapter 1

It is Sunday morning in the capital city of a British colony in West Africa, the Cathedral bell is ringing for matins and the people are on their way to church. Local colour is created by a few swift impressionistic touches: Negro schoolgirls; a bearded Indian fortune-teller; small boys soliciting the strolling naval officers from the convoy at anchor on behalf of their sisters; corrugated iron roofs; vultures 'as tame as domestic turkeys'.

Wilson, an accountant newly arrived from England, is sitting on the balcony of the Bedford Hotel, watching the passing crowd and waiting for his gin-and-bitters. We learn that he is striving to appear like a typical product of the English upper middle class and has a secret love of poetry. Presently he is joined by Harris, the cable censor, who helps him to beat off the advances of the Indian fortune-teller, expresses his hatred of life in the colony, and points out the passing figure of Scobie, the Deputy Commissioner of Police, a squat, grey-haired man. Harris informs Wilson that Scobie is reputed to sleep with black girls and has a wife with intellectual pretensions. He describes the colony as 'the original Tower of Babel' in the diversity of its racial groups, among whom the Syrians are believed to be the wealthiest and most powerful.

Down in the street, Scobie, the hero of the novel, is shown on a typical tour of the city, greeting an occasional passer-by and, later, fulfilling routine duties at the police station. With the description of his office we gain some knowledge of the man himself, with his love of simplicity and bareness and his knowledge of the colony. His wife has been with him since the phoney war, trapped in the colony. His only child, a little girl of nine, died three years earlier. Summoned by the Commissioner, who is due to retire, he learns officially that he has been passed over for promotion to the post; he appears unmoved, if apprehensive of his wife's reaction to the news. The Commissioner's high regard for his Deputy is obvious; he calls him 'Scobie the Just'. This judgment is borne out by Scobie's brief interview with a black girl who is complaining about ill-treatment from her landlady. The interview also leads the author to comment on his hero's methods of investigation, past and present; his relations with the natives; his suffering during a brief period of unpopularity; and his gradual integration—'he had begun to desire these people's trust and affection' (Bk. One, I, 1/2). We are not surprised to learn that such an honest man has been out-manoeuvred in the allocation of housing, losing his bungalow in Cape Station, the most prestigious quarter for Europeans, and being relegated to a square, one-storeyed house, built on a reclaimed swamp. For him this is a matter of indifference, for his wife a source of hurt pride.

We are now introduced to the latter, who is seen in sharp contrast to her husband, with her passion for accumulating objects; her desire to prove she has friends; her worldly ambition; her snobbery. Scobie is bound to his wife by pity more than love, and by a sense of responsibility for her happiness. Her very unattractiveness increases his compassion. We also meet Ali, the steward, a model of fidelity and competence, who has served Scobie attentively for fifteen years. After Scobie has calmed his wife's nerves with a blend of patience, tact and untruth, they prepare to go to the Club, she fearing the staring faces of the hostile members, he thinking of the Portuguese liner to be searched next day.

The Club is a perfect reflection of the English ruling class abroad, with its rules and rituals, petty snobbery, endless gossip and pointless drinking. The chief subject of discussion among its members on this occasion is the advisability of excluding Wilson (who has come as a guest) from membership, on the grounds that the admission of a mere accountant would lower the tone. We begin to understand the Commissioner's earlier description of them—'What a lot of swine they are, Scobie' (Bk. One, I, 1/2). Scobie meets Wilson, introduces him to Louise—successfully, because they have a common interest in poetry. But his pleasure is short-lived when he hears a junior officer refer disparagingly to Louise's literary pretensions. Secretly afraid that Louise will lose a newly-won friend by her patronising attitude, but enraged by the sneers of the others, Scobie demonstrates his affection for his wife publicly, but ineffectually. Wilson is invited to drop in for a drink on his way back; Scobie is to join them after his routine round of inspection.

Scobie's return home is delayed by an encounter with Yusef, a wily and powerful Syrian, who runs a chain of stores and is said to do a little diamond-smuggling on the side. Yusef's car has broken down, so Scobie gives him a lift to his home. Their conversation reveals their relationship at this stage: Yusef respects Sobie's integrity and longs for his friendship; Scobie has a sneaking liking for Yusef yet is determined to apply the law on all occasions. This encounter is half bantering, half serious, as they talk of Yusef's rival Tallit, diamond-smuggling, and Yusef's unique business methods. The widespread corruption touched on in this scene seems, paradoxically, to have strengthened Scobie's love of the place: 'Here you could love human beings nearly as God loved them, knowing the worst' (Bk. One, I, 1/5). Scobie then tours the dangerous quarter of the town, the wharves infested by rats, real and human, where the black policemen fear to go without white escort. His thoroughness and courage further demonstrate his competence and sense of duty as a policeman. On his brief call at the police station he informs the sergeant on duty that Fraser, the officer who had spoken slightingly of Louise at the Club, will not be required next day to inspect the liner. Fraser is thus deprived of the minor advantages of such an outing: a taste of good food and wine, and an opportunity to purchase gifts at the ship's store; and Scobie, surprisingly, is shown to be capable of mild revenge.

Scobie then returns home to find Wilson and Louise cementing their friendship by reading poetry together; cuts his hand and has it dressed by Ali (Louise cannot bear the sight of blood); indulges his love of privacy in the upstairs lavatory; and drives Wilson home. The sense of happiness induced by the acquisition of a friend for his wife is rudely shattered when he wakes early to find her in tears. His failure to be promoted, her growing hatred of the colony, her longing for a conventional English-style home and, more immediately, her desire to go to South Africa, have rendered her desperate. Despite his love of the colony and his revulsion at the thought of retirement he rashly promises to do what he can for her.

NOTES AND GLOSSARY:

matins: morning service

jigjig: slang term for copulation

The Golden Treasury: a well-known anthology of English poetry, first published in 1861

'Go on tell how ...': from 'The Nameless One' by James Clarence Mangan (1803–49)

U.A.C.: United Africa Company, a chain of British-owned stores in Africa

Gunga Din: the Indian hero of one of Rudyward Kipling's (1865–1936) poems. Used sarcastically by Fraser

Protectorate: former German colony which passed under British authority after the Treaty of Versailles

A lost thing: an allusion to 'The South Country', a poem by Hilaire Belloc (1870–1953)

Tower of Babel: biblical structure described in Genesis 11:4–9. After God had caused the builders to speak in a great many different languages, they no longer understood one another, and the tower was never completed

Mende:	a West African people
Aristides:	Athenian politician renowned for his integrity and sense of justice, nicknamed 'the just'
ladders . . . snakes:	a children's board game in which pictures of snakes and ladders retard, or accelerate, the players' progress. Usually called 'snakes and ladders'
'dashed':	bribed
palaver:	usually idle talk; here trouble or 'business'
blackwater fever:	an extreme form of malaria, usually fatal
Creole:	person of French or Spanish descent, born and raised in a tropical region
Canute:	eleventh-century King of England, who is supposed to have ordered the tide to stop advancing
atabrine:	an early cure for malaria which turned the skin yellow
Temne:	native of the inland part of Sierra Leone in Western Africa
humbug:	here trouble or physical inconvenience
Massa:	Negro speech for 'Master'
laterite:	clay, the surface of which hardens on exposure to the air
F.S.P.:	Field Service Police
goosegog:	British dialect form of 'gooseberry':
Lancing:	English public school, founded in 1848
A.D.C.:	aide-de-camp
Chistlehurst:	ultra-respectable suburb of London
Lady Bountiful:	a wealthy, patronising person, partly based on a character in George Farquhar's (1678–1707) *The Beaux Stratagem*
sah:	Negro speech for 'sir'
I had rather be . . . :	William Shakespeare's (1564–1616) *Henry IV*, Part 1, III.1.128. Hotspur, the man of action, is expressing his contempt for poetry

Chapter 2

Next morning he tries the conventional way of raising money by calling to see the bank manager, an eccentric hypochondriac; but meets with refusal on the grounds of war regulations. Despite the manager's kindness, he feels ashamed, humiliated by the refusal. Scobie then proceeds to the routine search of the Portuguese liner, the *Esperança*, after drinks and cigars with the Captain. He is tipped off about hidden letters and undertakes the unpleasant task of searching the Captain's cabin and turning over his very private possessions. In the bathroom he finds a letter in the cistern and the Captain breaks down, claiming it is a letter to his only daughter, containing nothing of political or financial interest. The discovery of a common Catholic faith intensifies the Captain's pleading; he then tries bribery—all apparently to no avail. Yet Scobie, affected by the pathos of the Captain's story and remembering his own only daughter, later opens the letter in defiance of all regulations and, convinced of its innocence and sincerity, tears it up and burns the pieces. He feels corrupted not by money but by sentiment. Mention of the daughter has been the turning point and thus the first step towards a loss of integrity has been taken.

He returns home wondering how he will break it to Louise that the trip to South Africa is no nearer. As anticipated, he meets tears and recriminations rising to the shrill accusation: 'You don't love me'. Bitter truths are spoken in the darkness and silence of the night and Scobie's strange character is further revealed: his longing for peace and solitude and his determination to protect his wife's happiness at all costs.

NOTES AND GLOSSARY:

navicert: a certificate exempting non-contraband goods from seizure or search

French letters: contraceptives

Lobito: port in Angola

school notice-board: where notices about scholastic, cultural and sporting activities are usually pinned up

My peace . . . :   St John 14:27

COMMENT: Part I of Book One is extremely dense. It sets the scene vividly and accurately with details about climate, fauna and flora, the mixture of races and the life of the British in their distant colony. All the main characters of the novel (except Helen), and many of the secondary ones, are presented and described. The hero, Scobie, is viewed from many angles: a conscientious and kindly police officer; a self-effacing but respected member of the British community; a believing Catholic; a loyal but unhappy husband. His dilemma is clear: he has to choose between disappointing his wife by not sending her to South Africa, and betraying his principles by raising money by doubtful means. The chief interest of the novel is now centred on his spiritual and moral evolution. How will he act?

BOOK ONE, PART II

Chapter 1

Wilson, preparing to dine at Tallit's house, receives a visit from Harris, who puts him right about what to wear: 'You don't have to dress for a Syrian, old man' (Bk. One, II, 1/1), and urges him to resign himself to having his fortune told in the bathroom by the turbaned Indian. The fortune-teller startles Wilson by speaking of his interest in poetry and his growing love for Louise; he suggests that Wilson, outwardly a mere accountant, may have another, more official function in the colony. Wilson agrees to join Harris in a game of cockroach-hunting when he returns that night.

Wilson meets Scobie, after a visit to the Commissioner's office, and is invited to spend the evening with the Scobies. A brief interview between Scobie and the Commissioner shows the former that Wilson is not quite what he seems.

NOTES AND GLOSSARY:

cummerbund:	waistband worn in place of a waistcoat in men's dress clothes
Bengal Lancer:	a film about the Indian Army under British rule
punkah:	a fanning device
The price of life:	an echo of Winston Churchill's (1874–1965) 'the price of liberty is eternal vigilance'
Picture Post:	an illustrated English weekly, now defunct
Queensbury:	the ninth Marquess of Queensberry (1844–1910) under whose auspices the rules for boxing were established

Chapter 2

Louise, Scobie and Wilson, returning to the Scobie home after a pre-dinner walk, during which Wilson makes advances to Louise, find Scobie preparing to go to Bamba, an outlying station, to deal with an emergency. Pemberton, the D.C. there, has committed suicide. Scobie urges Wilson to stay for a drink with Louise. Wilson becomes aware of strains in their relationship and we learn that he has kissed Louise in the disused station on the hill when, in the course of their walk, they sheltered there from the rain. This part ends with Scobie being driven off on the two-day trek and Wilson's feeling for Louise becoming stronger. Louise's solicitude for her husband is stressed, while the latter's high sense of duty and deep human understanding is counter-pointed by a seeming desire to throw her into Wilson's arms.

NOTES AND GLOSSARY:

D.C.: District Commissioner, in charge of an administrative area in West Africa

COMMENT: Part II is concerned mainly with Wilson. His rawness as a member of the British colony is brought out by Harris's advice about clothes and the rather obvious questions he asks at Tallit's house. Clearly he is a spy; but not a very subtle one. His sense of loneliness and interest in poetry have drawn him closer to Louise so that when Scobie leaves for Bamba something like an emotional triangle has been established. The comic side of the novel, provided mainly by Wilson and Harris, has been sketched in.

BOOK ONE, PART III

Chapter 1

Scobie's journey to Bamba is described, with Ali in faithful attendance. As ferries are crossed and villages left behind, he sleeps fitfully; wonders how he will raise the money to pay Louise's passage to South Africa, and thinks intermittently about Pemberton's suicide. Nevertheless, remembering similar journeys with Ali in the past, he feels almost happy, despite his conviction 'that no human being can really understand another, and no one can arrange another's happiness' (Bk. One, III, 1/1). Arriving at his destination, he goes first to see the Catholic priest, Father Clay, to find out what he can about the circumstances of Pemberton's suicide. From his talk with the distraught priest he goes on to the D.C.'s bungalow and is struck by the youth of the dead man. The immature letter left by Pemberton for his father causes Scobie to protest against the Church's hard teaching on the sin of suicide.

Scobie goes down with a dose of fever and sweats it out at the priest's house, tended by Ali. He is visited by Yusef who tells him of Pemberton's debts and again shows his respect for Scobie's integrity, while denying any part in the diamond-smuggling. Yusef seems to be warning Scobie against Wilson and Tallit and, guessing Scobie's need for money, proposes a loan at four per cent. The latter has confused dreams in which Pemberton's suicide and Louise's passage are intertwined.

He returns home to find the problem of Louise looming as large as ever, and conscious of her love for him, he decides against all reason to borrow the money from Yusef. Two weeks later Louise leaves by liner for South Africa after uneasy farewells and expressions of solicitude on both sides. Scobie returns home late and is visited by Yusef who asks him to take action against Tallit who is preparing, he says, to smuggle diamonds in the next Portuguese boat. Scobie holds out against Yusef; but we have the impression that he has lost some of his independence, that he is beginning to pay, in terms of self-respect and even of rectitude, for borrowing money from Yusef.

NOTES AND GLOSSARY:

styx-like: hellish, gloomy (from Styx, in classical mythology a river in the underworld)

Little Flower: affectionate name for Saint Teresa of Lisieux (1873–97)

Somerset Maugham: (1874–1965) an English playwright, novelist and short-story writer; he was very widely read, especially in the first half of the twentieth century

Edgar Wallace: (1875–1932) a prolific writer of detective stories who was a very successful best-selling author between the two world wars

Sydney Horler: a popular but second-rate author of thrillers in the 1920s and 1930s

peine forte et dure: torture sanctioned by medieval law in order to extract information

a Daniel: biblical character noted for wisdom and uprightness

IOU's: 'I owe you', a written acknowledgement of a debt

jiggers: familiar form of 'chigger', a blood-sucking, disease-carrying insect of African origin

Oxford Verse: *The Oxford Book of English Verse*, a well-known anthology of English poetry (1900)

the Woolfs: works by Virginia Woolf (1882–1941), English novelist and critic; her husband Leonard Woolf (1880–1969) was a publisher and political writer

paw-paw: oblong, yellowish tropical fruit

bow-wows: polite slang for 'bowels'

helio: telegraphing apparatus

The Prophet: Mohammed

Lagos: capital of Nigeria

Vichy French: those supporting the Pétain regime during the second World War

COMMENT: In Part III the main interest is once again centred on Scobie, the hero. His expedition into the bush with Ali must be a near-replica of many previous journeys. After the routine examination of the circumstances of Pemberton's suicide, he contracts fever and is waited on by the faithful Ali with the skill and tenderness of a devoted nurse; he receives a visit from Yusef. Obsessed by young Pemberton's tragic end and by the problem of Louise's passage to South Africa, he seems better armed to question the Church's teaching about suicide than to resist Yusef's tempting offer of a loan. This scene heralds Scobie's future fate vividly: he is going to put himself in Yusef's power and he is going to plan his own suicide as a solution to his problems. Louise's departure for South Africa and Yusef's nocturnal visit to his home serve to emphasise Scobie's changed circumstances. Altogether this part foreshadows the future with remarkable skill.

BOOK TWO, PART I

Chapter 1

At Pende, Scobie and the local D.C., Perrot, are waiting for the survivors of a torpedoed ship to be brought over from the French side of the river. Wilson is also there, ostensibly to inspect the U.A.C. store. There is talk about the discovery of diamonds smuggled in a parrot's crop on one of the Portuguese ships. Is Tallit the guilty party, or Yusef? Scobie, spending the night with the Perrots, keeps his diary, and, according to habit, prays before falling asleep. The next morning the survivors are brought across from the opposite shore: a Scotch engineer, two elderly men, a spinster called Miss Malcott. A French officer arrives in the launch with seven stretcher cases, including a boy of ten and a little girl who seems to be dying—after forty days in an open boat. Scobie starts wondering how her fate can be reconciled with the love of God; but the officer's account of the self-sacrifice of the others on her behalf seems to him to offer an explanation. He then sees another survivor—still nameless—a young woman of nineteen whose husband has been lost: she is lying on a stretcher with her eyes shut, tightly clasping a stamp-album. Later the doctor gives Scobie news of the survivors and the latter again muses on the human condition: 'What an absurd thing it was to expect happiness in a world so full of misery .... If one knew, he wondered, the facts, would one have to feel pity even for the planets? if one reached what they called *the heart of the matter*' (Bk. Two, I, 1/3).

At the request of Mrs Bowles, the missionary's wife, Scobie is left alone with the little girl in the temporary hospital. He witnesses her death, overcome by the recollection of his own dead daughter and the tragedy of suffering parenthood. He decides to stay on at Pende in case of other deaths; avoids the child's funeral; and is again recruited by Mrs Bowles, this time to read to the schoolboy, now in the same ward as the young woman. The choice of books at the Mission is limited to mawkish Victorian literature, mainly religious; but Scobie manages to turn one of these, *A Bishop among the Bantus*, into an exciting adventure story likely to appeal to a normal schoolboy. He makes the acquaintance of the other occupant of the ward, Mrs Rolt (the young woman with the stamp album), who is still weak after her ordeal.

Wilson, who has been inspecting the store, questions Scobie's integrity and malevolently suggests that Yusef is 'protected'. Enraged by Scobie's self-possession and cruel mockery of his declared love for Louise, he loses control, accuses Scobie of jealousy and even suggests the latter has a special interest in Mrs Rolt. Faced with the Deputy Commissioner's unflinching calm and paternal charity, Wilson breaks down in tears in front of his hated rival.

NOTES AND GLOSSARY:

Pende:	district in what is now Central African Republic
France:	that is, territory under French rule
Allan Quatermain:	hero of several of Sir Henry Rider Haggard's (1856–1925) novels, notably *She*
***Timbres*:**	(*French*) stamps
Cities of the Plain:	in the Bible Sodom and Gomorrah, destroyed because of their depravity (Genesis 19)
***Treasure Island*:**	the famous adventure story by Robert Louis Stevenson
rakehelly:	wicked-looking
show . . . a clean pair of heels:	escape untouched
the colonial sport:	through boredom, members of the colony might indulge in love affairs

Chapter 2

Some weeks later Scobie meets Mrs Rolt again when he goes to inspect one of the Nissen huts which is showing a light during black-out. He discovers that she has been discharged from hospital and given temporary lodging there. He stays for a drink and, whereas others had intimidated her by pressing their sympathy on her, he draws her out about her childhood in Bury St Edmunds, her schooldays, the mistresses who taught her, games and other school activities. His understanding of her situation—a young woman, widowed in tragic circumstances, who has survived a terrible ordeal by sea—is remarkable: he realises that she needs just to talk about ordinary, everyday things. They part as friends. The next morning he deals with routine cases at the station, writes to his wife and is summoned by the Commissioner, whom he finds flanked by the Colonial Secretary and the M.I.5 representative, Colonel Wright, up specially from Cape Town. Scobie is questioned by the latter two about the smuggled diamonds and it is suggested that he is receiving hush money from Yusef. He leaves them in anger, determined to have it out with Yusef.

On the way to see Yusef he gives a lift to Harris who is doubly excited because he has found a hut to share with Wilson and has discovered (through a mention of his own name in the school magazine) that he and Wilson were at the same school, Downham. Harris shows Scobie the letter he has drafted to the secretary of the school magazine and declares that he was never happy at school. Scobie find Yusef asleep in the little room where he had borrowed money from the Syrian to pay for Louise's passage to South Africa. Yusef confesses to 'framing' Tallit, threatens to go to the Commissioner with the whole story and finally pleads for Scobie's friendship. On his way home Scobie goes to confession, where his main sin seems to be a partial loss of faith.

NOTES AND GLOSSARY:

total black-out: reference to wartime regulations, according to which all lights had to be concealed because of danger of air raids

Heights of Abraham: a reference to the battle which won Canada from the French for the British in 1759, through the victory of General Wolfe over Montcalm

Nissen: prefabricated shelter of corrugated iron, with cement floor

All clear: signal that the air raid danger had passed

schwarmerei: an excessive sentimental regard

totem-pole: carved pole with totemic symbols of religious significance

cui bono **principle:** assigning responsibility to the person who stood to gain from the action or crime

red cloth waves: the moment of danger, a reference to bull-fighting

Pimpernel: in the novel *The Scarlet Pimpernel* by Baroness Orczy (1865–1942), a secret agent who acted on behalf of the 'ancien régime' during the French Revolution

Downhamian: school magazine of the school, Downham

Ivanhoe: one of Sir Walter Scott's (1771–1832) most famous historical novels

coaster: resident on a sea coast

lost his integrity: where he had borrowed money from Yusef

lacy altar in Ealing: reference to his wedding service at Ealing, in West London

Royal Ordnance: branch of the British Army responsible for procuring and distributing supplies

Kru: indigenous black people of Liberia

gets you down: depresses you

hocus pocus: a meaningless formula used to cloak deception

Chapter 3

Scobie visits Helen Rolt with a gift of stamps for her album. She talks about her dead husband, he tells her the circumstances of his child's death; and thus their feeling for one another is cemented. Scobie is moved by her youth and inexperience: she seems helpless to him. They discuss the future, have a drink together, and look at the stamps. Flight-Lieutenant Bagster, who has earlier been making advances to her at the beach, comes knocking at the door. Receiving no answer, he moves on and, clinging to one another, they kiss and become lovers: 'What they had both thought was safety, proved to have been the camouflage of an enemy who works in terms of friendship, trust and pity' (Bk. Two, I, 3/1).

Scobie leaves her at 4 a.m. for reasons of discretion, but forgets his umbrella. When he wakes at home after a brief sleep he feels cast down at the thought of this new 'responsibility'. He has no illusions about the situation: he knows in advance the unhappiness and pain his relationship with Helen will bring to him and to others. He also feels he has betrayed God.

NOTES AND GLOSSARY:
George V: King of England (1856–1936)
A.T.S., W.A.A.F.: Auxiliary Territorial Service, Women's Auxiliary Air Force

COMMENT: Chapter 1 shows us the impact of the war on the colony and introduces us to Helen Rolt, from now on one of the main figures in the story. Scobie's character takes on a new dimension as we witness his feeling for human suffering generally and his (very different) ways of dealing with the two children. Wilson overreaches himself by accusing Scobie of corruption and by dramatising his own relations with Louise. He is less comic than contemptible. In Chapter 2 Scobie sees Helen Rolt for the second time; she is now established in a Nissen hut close to his house. Her youth and inexperience awake in him feelings of pity and protectiveness; his kindness and understanding draw her towards him. The stage is set for love. After a routine morning of petty cases, Scobie has an unpleasant interview with the Colonial Secretary and the M.I.5 representative, in the presence of the Commissioner, during which it is suggested that his relations with Yusef are irregular. He defends himself with dignity but also with rising anger, and afterwards has a showdown with Yusef. Feeling spiritually empty he seeks the comfort of confession, without much effect. In Chapter 3 Scobie and Helen become lovers on his second visit to her Nissen hut, drawn together by loneliness and loss but also by a strong mutual affection, based partly on pity on his side, partly on gratitude on hers. Described by one critic as 'the saddest seduction in modern literature' this affair can only multiply Scobie's problems and make him infinitely more vulnerable. He is now responsible for the happiness of two women and, given his Catholic faith, faces a burden of guilt into the bargain.

BOOK TWO, PART II

Chapter 1

This chapter provides some light relief with Harris and Wilson settling into their new home and the former discovering a love poem by the latter (addressed to Louise) in *The Downhamian*. Wilson sees Scobie in the middle of the night, obviously returning from a visit to Helen. We watch Wilson at his secret work on the codes and interviewing Yusef's boy, whom he has decided to pay for information. Tired of decoding, and of the contradictory messages that seem to arrive, Wilson departs to pay a visit to the local brothel. Once inside he feels reluctance, even revulsion, and tries to withdraw; but the old mammy compels him to stay and extracts the fee, in a scene which is rich in comedy.

NOTES AND GLOSSARY:

snakey ....Jagger's House ....Progs:	schoolboy slang from their old school, Downham
extra halves:	additional half days off
unlicked:	revealing youthful naiveté or crude manners
Harpenden:	presumably a neighbouring school
crockets:	architectural ornaments of curved foliage
sod:	short for 'sodomite', used as general term of abuse
narrow squeak:	close escape
old lag:	established convict
on the halls:	performing in the music halls
mangroves:	mangrove is a common tropical tree
pinpoint:	make conspicuous

COMMENT: This shift in interest to a secondary intrigue is a welcome break in the tension created by Scobie's problems. Wilson, the romantic poet, is revealed as a sordid sensualist, and this sexual interlude serves to highlight the purity of the feeling that unites Scobie and Helen.

BOOK TWO, PART III

Chapter 1

During Scobie's third visit to Helen she accuses him of putting her second; of taking no risks. She reproaches him bitterly, ignoring his attempts to soothe her, and finally tells him to go and never return. Conscious that this would be a solution to his problems, but bound to her by pity and love, he returns home and writes her a letter in which he commits himself entirely. He slips it under her door, thinking that she will not be able to accuse him of being too cautious now. He receives a call from Father Rank who enquires after Louise and confesses his own sense of frustration and failure as a priest, both in England earlier and now in the colony. He seems to be appealing to Scobie for help and encouragement. On his way to dinner with the Commissioner, Scobie finds that Wilson has visited his office in his absence and, perhaps, looked at his files. He faces the Commissioner with Wilson's double identity, informs him of his loan from Yusef, and in return receives a much-needed assurance of confidence. It is clear, despite the Commissioner's lack of action, that he and Scobie are linked by the same conception of service, the same understanding of the colony and its people, the same basic decency.

This brief conversation emphasises their mutual affection and respect and does much to restore Scobie's morale. Despite Helen's bitter dismissal he returns to the hut, to find her remorseful and loving. But their reunion is spoiled by the discovery that Scobie's letter has never reached her, with the attendant dangers of blackmail or denunciation. Scobie returns home at once to find a telegram from his wife announcing her imminent return. Recalling that he promised Helen that he would always be there if she needed him, he feels doubly committed, a victim of people who have calls on his pity. He tries to pray but realises that he is asking too much of God: happiness for other people as well as peace for himself. He has thoughts of suicide but pulls himself together, makes the usual succinct diary entry, and prepares to meet a dangerous future.

NOTES AND GLOSSARY:

the hard swearing . . . :	adolescent girls trying to show they are grown up
twister:	a tricky, unprincipled person
Northampton:	city in the centre of England
clapper:	tongue of a bell
tumbled to it:	discovered the truth of the position
bitched:	treated as a woman without principles would
slutted:	behaved immorally

Chapter 2

Obsessed by thoughts of the telegram from his wife during the pursuit of his duties, Scobie accepts an invitation to dinner from Fellowes, the sanitary inspector. Arriving there he finds Helen among the guests and they behave as if they hardly knew one another. Conversation at dinner turns to the Pemberton case and to suicide generally. Scobie finds an opportunity of speaking to Helen alone and breaks the news of his wife's imminent return. He declares: 'I shall never again want any home without you' (Bk. Two, III, 2/1). The evening ends with the usual exchange of courtesies. Scobie returns home to find Yusef waiting for him, *and* a letter from Helen. The letter, which releases him from any promises, is so full of love and self-sacrifice that he has difficulty in concentrating on Yusef's business. It turns out that Yusef is asking him to deliver a small packet to the Captain of the *Esperança*, due to call at the port in a couple of days. When the claims of 'friendship' prove insufficient, he threatens to have Scobie's letter to Helen (which has come into his possession) delivered to Louise as soon as she lands. In the brief routine search of the *Esperança* that follows Scobie discovers that the Captain is the one he already knows. He receives a friendly welcome tempered by pity, when the Captain finds that Scobie too is acting illegally: he wonders if he is now a man for whom people feel pity.

NOTES AND GLOSSARY:

chop:	British slang for food
stigmata:	painful marks, reference to Christ's wounds
angina:	a painful heart disease with suffocating effects
shuttlecock:	the feathered cork volleyed to and fro in the game of badminton
serius:	mis-spelling of 'serious'
hore:	mis-spelling of 'whore'
bare:	Yusef means 'skinned' of course
the base Indian:	refers to Othello's last speech in Act V. 2 of Shakespeare's tragedy of the same name
boom:	chain cable to protect the harbour mouth

COMMENT: In Part III of Book Two the action moves faster. Helen, showing the strains of a clandestine love affair, reproaches Scobie with undue caution and he, to prove the strength of his feeling, unwisely sends her a passionate love letter, which never reaches her. Scobie's brief interviews with Father Rank and the Commissioner only serve to stress the high standards of behaviour people expect of him. The lost letter to Helen and the news of Louise's return increase his dilemma tenfold, Helen's tender, forgiving letter and Yusef's blackmailing both put him more in their power, in different ways. It is difficult to see how he can extricate himself from a situation in which his integrity as a policeman, his honour as a husband and his orthodoxy as a Catholic have been impaired.

BOOK THREE, PART I

Chapter 1

Scobie goes out to meet Louise on the liner that has brought her back from South Africa. He finds her alone in the large cabin (from which the other women have discreetly withdrawn) and feels embarrassed by their words of greeting and her declared resolution to behave differently. As her bags are being unpacked and the photograph of the dead child in the white Communion veil replaced in the bedroom, the old feeling of pity returns very strongly and his love for Helen seems temporarily remote, even unreal. His wife's wish to go to Communion with him the next day poses a new and terrible problem, for Communion will have to be preceded by Confession, which will imply the termination of his affair with Helen. His wife is struck by his jocularity, which is in fact a defence against despair.

Using a visit to Wilson as a pretext, Scobie goes to see Helen but finds her quite unable to grasp the gravity of his dilemma as a Catholic. With innocent cruelty she even suggests that it may well be an excuse for leaving her. Yet Scobie's strongest feeling, in her presence, is his determination to protect her from suffering.

The next morning Scobie is unable to face an act so blasphemous as taking Communion in a state of mortal sin; so he simulates a heart attack and takes a sip of brandy in front of Louise, which (at that time) was enough in itself to exclude Communion.

NOTES AND GLOSSARY:

to rattle:	to upset
ectoplasm:	emanation from a medium, here used metaphorically
crack:	jest
squire of dames:	ladies' man
hung for a sheep:	from the proverb 'You might as well be hung for a sheep as for a lamb', that is, 'as you are going to be punished for a small misdeed, you might as well commit a more serious one'
hooey:	nonsense
Hotspur:	character in Shakespeare's Henry IV, Part I

sweat-lank: hanging straight, damp with sweat
domine non sum dignus: (*Latin*) O Lord, I am not worthy

Chapter 2

Wilson comes to see Louise with his school magazine poem, deter-mined to declare his love. But everything falls flat; the poem is not at all to her taste, the reference to the kisses in the disused station months before shows her indifference; his declaration of love evokes mockery almost equal to Scobie's earlier taunt: she explains his love as 'Coast fever'. Stung to anger by her blatant lack of interest, he hits back by linking Scobie's name with Helen's and receives a blow in the face for his pains. Recovering from a bleeding nose, he continues the discussion stretched out on the floor; and implies that Scobie is being used by Yusef. His undignified position is emphasised by the arrival of Scobie himself and the casual courtesy of the latter's queries. He withdraws, mortally offended, an object of contempt to all concerned.

Louise gives her husband a brief account of what has happened and then reiterates her request that he should accompany her to Commun-ion. Feeling caught, and in the full knowledge of what he should do as a Catholic, he goes to Confession, tortured by the hopelessness of his position. Father Rank offers no solution he does not know of already, so he goes to Mass with his wife the next morning determined to reassure her. There follows, in church, another of those internal debates which mark the novel. Up to the last moment we wonder how he will act. Finally he puts the happiness of others (as he sees it) before his own salvation and the irrevocable act is committed: he takes Com-munion in a state of sin.

NOTES AND GLOSSARY:

Coast fever:	a temporary love affair indulged in out of boredom
'O lyric love . . .':	from *The Ring and the Book* by Robert Browning (1812–89)
Seconds:	men who assist a duellist or boxer
rake up:	remember with difficulty
Milosis:	hidden city in Sir Henry Rider Haggard's *Allan Quatermain* (1887)
hidden stakes:	concealed trap
Kyrie Eleison:	(*Greek*) prayer at Mass—'Lord have mercy'

Chapter 3

Scobie calls on the bank manager and asks to see his medical encyclopaedia, remembering that at the Fellowes dinner party Dr

Sykes had suggested the best way of committing suicide would be to have a prescription for angina. He wants to note the symptoms for a future which is beginning to take shape in his mind. He then learns from the Commissioner that after all he *is* to succeed to the top job. (The chosen candidate is being sent elsewhere.) He realises, too late, that all his deflections from duty, moral and professional, need never have happened: 'If Louise had stayed I should never have loved Helen: I would never have been blackmailed by Yusef, never have committed that act of despair' (Bk. Three, I, 3/1). He therefore reacts unenthusiastically to the news and lets it be understood that his health is bad, thereby conditioning people in advance to the subsequent news of his death.

At the car he sees his steward talking to a small boy who, it transpires, works for Wilson; and though Ali reassures him of his loyalty, a seed of doubt in Scobie's mind is sown: as he himself has lied, so can others. He brings some furniture to Helen's hut, tells her the news of his appointment but finds her bitter and full of recriminations. Shaken out of his usual calm, he loses his temper and tries to make her understand the gravity of his action in taking Communion while in a state of mortal sin. Her response is petty and uncomprehending at first; but at the idea that he may be ill, her tenderness returns. He takes her for a drive and when they kiss goodbye in the garage, Ali appears in the shadows. Once again Scobie wonders whether his steward is absolutely trustworthy.

Returning home, he makes his usual brief diary entry and suddenly feels the weight of loneliness, with nobody to confide in and nobody able to understand his predicament fully. As if to add to his burden, Yusef's boy arrives surreptitiously with the gift of a diamond, is caught by Ali and thrown out. Conscious of all Ali knows, Scobie doubts his incorruptibility for the third time.

Louise from upstairs calls to remind him not to drink after midnight, the next day being All Saints' Day; and he has a vision of all the future days on which *he* will be betraying God. Has Ali been betraying *him*? he wonders.

NOTES AND GLOSSARY:

stuff and nonsense:	something quite silly
sternum:	breastbone
Coriolanus:	Shakespeare's hero of the tragedy of the same name who, through pride, refused to exhibit his wounds
like Caesar:	she means 'like Caesar's wife'
a quiet dog:	slang term for sly fellow
Midnight Mass:	the service to usher in Christmas

Chapter 4

On his way to make a late call on Yusef, Scobie meets Wilson, who again accuses him of not appreciating his wife, and this time admits to spying activities. Strangely drawn to Yusef, Scobie confides to him his doubts about Ali and about the link between Ali and Wilson through the small boy. Yusef promises to settle the question and his boy is sent to bring Ali to them. Yusef leaves Scobie temporarily to 'give instructions' and the latter begins to entertain fears about the means to be employed. They talk on through the night till a cry of pain and fear is heard and Scobie, galvanised into action, rushes out down the dangerous wharf to find Ali lying there, murdered. He is overcome by guilt, remorse and grief.

NOTES AND GLOSSARY:
very quiet like the grave: African variation of 'as quiet as the grave'
nursery peace: the protection given to young children
a millstone: a burden of guilt

COMMENT: As events move at a faster pace in this part, suspense is heightened. How will Scobie manage to maintain his love for two women without making one of them suffer? How will he continue to reconcile his Catholic faith with taking Communion in a state of mortal sin? How will his loss of trust in Ali affect his actions? His affair with Helen degenerates under her recriminations and his ever-present pity. His relations with Louise acquire a new dimension in the light of his infidelity and their shared Catholic faith. His ambiguous relationship with Yusef leads to the death of Ali. Meanwhile Wilson continues his spying activities and does little to add to his dignity as lover or man.

BOOK THREE, PART II

Chapter 1

The next day Scobie, overcome by the circumstances of Ali's death, resolves yet again to put his affairs in order and start anew. After work, he drives up to the Nissen hut to end his affair with Helen and meets her, distraught, coming down the hill. Shaken by the news of Ali's death and its implications for Scobie, she declares *her* decision to leave *him*, despite her deep love. Beneath her passion and tenderness there is an astonishing understanding of the real man: 'You'll be a Catholic again—that's what you really want, isn't it, not a pack of women?' (Bk. Three, II, 1/1). During her long monologue he keeps thinking that if he were dead, she would be free of him and could forget him. Before their farewell scene is over he has made up his mind to take his own life as the only possible solution to his problems.

Almost immediately we see him with Louise, who is conventionally sympathetic about Ali but rejuvenated at the thought of becoming the Commissioner's wife and already planning a Christmas party. Scobie is revolted by what seems her smugness and thinks, characteristically, 'it was the hysterical woman who felt the world laughing behind her back that I loved. I love failure: I can't love success' (Bk. Three, II, 1/2). But love replaces hatred when he realises that Louise will never be the Commissioner's wife. Later he writes up his diary, adding entries for the past week about sleeplessness so as to render his future action more plausible.

NOTES AND GLOSSARY:
clean up: put life in order
dithering: trembling with agitation
unrepentant thief: one of the thieves crucified with Christ

Chapter 2

Scobie visits Dr Travis, as planned, gets a tentative diagnosis of angina and a prescription for a strong sleeping-draught to cure his alleged sleeplessness. Realising yet again that the happiness of others has to be protected, he proceeds to plan his suicide scientifically: as this is the worst crime a Catholic could commit he wants to take the greatest care over it.

Before announcing his retirement to the Commissioner, he stops at the church and, unable to pray, holds something like a dialogue with God in which he pleads his guilt and his despair and his sense of responsibility; and the answering voice begs for trust and time. But Scobie's mind is made up: he turns his back on the altar and leaves the church.

NOTES AND GLOSSARY:
Evipan: a form of anaesthetic, used as pain killer
blob: a small drop or lump
Golgotha: the hill near Jerusalem where Christ was crucified

Chapter 3

Scobie's diary for early November reveals a mixture of routine duties, social engagements and references to his state of health. Having put aside a dose every night for nine nights, he is now ready, on 12 November, to take the fatal overdose. He visits Helen's hut for the last time, finds her out and leaves a message of love in the stamp album. At dinner he deliberately discusses future plans with his wife and, unwilling to let her go for ever, asks her to read poetry at bedtime. A last view of her fills him with the old pitying feeling and love.

After a conventional goodnight and his usual assurance that he loves her, Louise goes up to bed, leaving him to his final solitude. Thrusting aside an inner voice which urges him to go on with his ordinary life, Scobie swallows the tablets. After an abortive attempt to pray, and a pathetic appeal to Ali, he feels someone is calling to him for help and he struggles to his feet, only to crash to the ground, unconscious.

NOTES AND GLOSSARY:
play-acting: insincere or theatrical behaviour

COMMENT: Shocked and grieved by Ali's death, Scobie determines to clear up the mess of his life; but, in his meeting with Helen, love and pity are stronger than resolve; and suicide seems the only way out of his dilemma. His decision made, the old protective feeling for Louise, whose hopes of a happy future are groundless, returns; and he proceeds carefully and firmly to plan his death 'from angina' with visits to the doctor and the Commissioner, and careful entries in his diary to allay any suspicion of suicide. Despite the voice of conscience and the Church's view of suicide, he takes the necessary overdose, thus conclusively ending his life as husband and lover and policeman, and jeopardising his spiritual future. It is left to the others to reconstruct the truth and to write his epitaph.

BOOK THREE, PART III

Chapter 1

This brief concluding part, consisting of one short chapter, gives us a glimpse of what happens *after the end*. Wilson, in his double capacity as lover and spy, comes to call on Louise: ostensibly a visit of sympathy, it quickly turns into an investigation of the circumstances of Scobie's death. The additional entries about sleeplessness (in darker ink) and the careful record of his taking Evipan make it clear that angina was *not* the cause of his death. Left with this horror, Louise seeks comfort from Father Rank whose words go straight to the heart of the matter: 'He never had any trust in mercy—except for other people .... The Church knows all the rules. But it doesn't know what goes on in a single human heart' (Bk. Three, III, 1/3). In a sense the novel has been an attempt to explore just this.

In concluding his novel on this controversial note, Graham Greene is demonstrating his unorthodoxy, his determination to pit his own convictions against the traditional teaching of the Church. These last pages may well serve as a questioning of certain tenets of the Catholic faith. Above all they are an assertion of the supreme power of divine love.

NOTES AND GLOSSARY:

pickled: slightly drunk
prang: slang term for fornication
dodo: extinct bird

Part 3

Commentary

Structure and plot

The novel is divided into three books, each consisting of three parts. Each part contains a differing number of chapters which, in turn, are divided into a varying number of subsections. This somewhat elaborate structure makes the work a little confusing for reference; but in fact it is tightly organised and economically written. The story covers a period of several months; but reaches back over several years (Harris remembering his schooldays (Bk. Two, I, 2/3); Father Rank recalling his parish in Northampton (Bk. Two, III, 1/2); Scobie returning frequently to his wedding at Ealing and to the death of his little girl years before).

In his introduction to the revised edition of 1971, the author expressed some dissatisfaction with the story. 'The scales to me seem too heavily weighted, the plot overloaded, the religious scruples of Scobie too extreme.' He therefore re-inserted, for technical reasons, the scene between Mrs Scobie and Wilson on their evening walk along the abandoned railway track, which occurs in Book One, Part II, Chapter 2/1 and which, to quote the author again, 'put Mrs Scobie's character in a more favourable light'.

Skilful use is made of parallel events: Tallit's dinner party in Book One, Part II and Fellowes's dinner party in Book Two, Part III; Pemberton's suicide early on and Scobie's suicide at the end; the little girl's death at Pende and Scobie's daughter's death years before—the first before Scobie's eyes, the second in his absence. Scobie's letter to his wife is neatly contrasted with his letter to Helen. Everything that happens is closely linked to the main plot, building up the pressure on the hero, increasing the pace of the narrative, illuminating the nature of the chief characters.

Setting

In a brief preface the author tells us that 'The geographical background of the story is drawn from that part of West Africa of which I have had personal experience'. The colony is thus brought to life, with descriptions of its climate—rainy season, sweltering sun, heavy dampness; its fauna—pye dogs and vultures, mosquitoes and cockroaches, lizards and 'jiggers'; its mixture of races—Africans (whether Temne or Mende), Indians, Creoles, Syrians, a cross-section of British people, brief appearances by a Portuguese captain and a French officer; its diseases—malaria and blackwater fever. The port, with Portuguese liners calling and its short-lived sunset beauty, the laterite roads and Nissen huts, the swamps and the low hills, the wharf squalor, all serve to evoke the scene vividly.

British presence

Inevitably it is the British presence that dominates this British colony, with its Law Courts and police stations; its gin and bitters and habit of dressing for dinner; its social code and petty snobbery (Wilson becomes socially acceptable when Fellowes discovers that the former's old school used to play a match against his own – Bk. Two, III, 2/1. The old school tie and the public school ethos generally are much in evidence: Fellowes 'fingering for confidence the Lancing tie' (Bk. One, I, 1/4); Harris discovering the *Old Downhamian* (Bk. Two, I, 2/3); social distinctions at the Club; the English disapproval of any public show of feeling—'A chap's got the right to take his own life, of course, but there's no need for fuss' (Bk. Two, III, 2/1). Above all there is the widespread xenophobia: against the Syrians (Bk. One, II, 1/1), against the French (Bk. Two, I, 1/1), against the blacks (Bk. Three, I, 3/2). All these attitudes reflect a sense of racial superiority, from which only Scobie seems immune.

War background

As Graham Greene himself tells us, the novel is based on first-hand experience of Sierra Leone during the war, in 1942–3; and indeed the war is present from first to last, obvious in the ever-present danger of air raids or armed invasion, in the censorship of letters, in the searching of neutral ships at 'an important harbour', in the proximity of the Vichy French, in the enforcement of black-outs, and so on. Ships are frequently sunk, expected supplies fail to arrive, leave is curtailed. More significantly, the circumstances of the story arise from war conditions. Louise had joined Scobie during the first year of the phoney war and was unable to return to England later because of the danger of submarines. Her unhappiness in the colony induces him to borrow money from Yusef to pay for her passage to South Africa, a decision fraught with threats to his incorruptibility as a police officer. In peace-time he would doubtless have been able to borrow from his bank; as it is, the bank manager cannot help him because of war regulations about overdrafts. Furthermore, Helen enters the story (and

Scobie's life) when he goes to Pende to receive the survivors of a torpedoed ship. Scobie's dilemma—caught between two women—is thus
directly caused by the war conditions. Lastly, it is the diamond
smuggling which causes the further breaches in the hero's integrity and
indeed explains Wilson's presence in the town, engaged as he is (however ineffectively) in M.I.5 activities. The shadow of the war hangs
over the novel, increasing the suspense, conditioning the behaviour of
the characters and making life in the colony more exciting and more
explosive than it would otherwise have been.

The religious theme

The place of the Catholic Church in the story and Scobie's attachment
to his faith are never in doubt; they colour the whole novel. The framework of Catholicism is emphasised by the presence of a practising
Catholic couple in a community where most of the white people we see
are either agnostics or wishy-washy Anglicans; by the presence of two
priests—Father Rank and Father Clay—and the recollection of a third,
Père Brûle (Bk. Two, I, 1/2); by the frequent use of Christian imagery
(Golgotha, for example, and the unrepentant thief) and by many quot-
ations from the Bible and the Mass. We accompany Scobie twice to the
confessional and twice to Mass; we witness his private prayers (Bk.
Two, I, 1/1) and his meditations in church (Bk. Three, II, 2/1).

Apart from these formal reminders, there are many references and
remarks which demonstrate the significance of the Catholic faith
within the story: as when the Portuguese captain discovers that Scobie
is a Catholic (Bk. One, I, 2/2); or when Louise says bitterly about
Helen—'But she's not a Catholic. She's lucky. She's free' (Bk. Three,
I, 2/1); or when Scobie reminds Helen that he cannot marry her
because of his religious principles (Bk. Two, III, 1/1). Moreover the
hero himself is constantly stressing his faith or querying its doctrine on
specific issues—Pemberton's suicide or the purity of love ('against all
the teaching of the Church, one has the conviction that love—any kind
of love—does deserve a bit of mercy' (Bk. Three, I, 1/1). Indeed
Father Rank himself continues the argument after Scobie's suicide:
'The Church knows all the rules. But it doesn't know what goes on in a
single human heart' (Bk. Three, III, 1/3).

It is Scobie's religious dilemma, as much as the pity and responsibility he feels for others, that guides his actions, colours his thoughts
and reveals his personality throughout the book. Had he not been a
believing Catholic, there would have been no deadlock, no internal
struggle, virtually none of the suspense that holds the interest from
first to last. Despite the author's own assertion about Scobie's salvation or damnation not being an issue in the novel (revised 1971

edition, pp. XIV, XV), the story grips us largely because of its religious theme and the hero's spiritual anguish; his knowledge that suicide is the unforgivable sin, his conviction that taking communion in a state of mortal sin means damnation. Reduced to Catholic terms, his problem is that Communion is impossible without Confession and that Confession is impossible without giving up Helen, whom he has promised to love and protect (Bk. Three, I, 1/1).

Greeneland

Critics have used this term to designate the physical framework and moral climate which seem to characterise the novels of Graham Greene. 'Greeneland' has come to suggest a place where ugliness, sordidity and seediness predominate; where there is a notable absence of lasting pleasure and noble behaviour. The author had read T.S. Eliot's (1888–1965) 'The Waste Land' at the impressionable age of eighteen and, like many of his contemporaries, been profoundly influenced by its picture of the decay and moral rottenness prevailing in the modern world. While 'The Waste Land' also reflected a hankering after a nobler, purer, more heroic past, Greene's own form of nostalgia is rather for a return to barbarism, so that mankind can start anew at the point where things began to go wrong. This nostalgia had already been expressed in his love for the Indians in Mexico (*The Lawless Roads*, *The Power and The Glory*) and in his declared view in the thirties that Abyssinia 'was perhaps more worth preserving than the bright, slick, streamlined civilisation threatening it'. Furthermore, he says, man-made solutions are doomed to failure and human justice often arbitrary (Scobie is the exception, not the rule). Communism, Capitalism, Fascism and Socialism are rejected because they are 'based on what we are'. Happiness is an illusion, love means 'pain suffered and pain inflicted'. As a result any symptoms of a breakdown in modern civilisation are eagerly sought after by the author; ugliness, decay and sordidity welcomed, almost gleefully. This is so whatever the setting: Africa, Asia, South America, England or Continental Europe. The conventional sources of happiness and fulfilment – love, beauty, culture, friendship, a noble cause, etc. – are largely excluded.

The Heart of the Matter is no exception, with its descriptions of ugliness (Nissen huts, laterite roads, government furniture) and decay (scratched enamel, dirty soap, broken rosary). The constant presence of vultures, rats and dead pye dogs adds a sinister note. Human beings are rarely seen at their best, witness Fraser and Wilson hunting cockroaches, Louise sweating under the mosquito net, Yusef biting his nails ('snip, snip, snip'), the tipsy Bagster's lecherous advances to Helen. In recounting Scobie's tour of the wharf (early on), the Portuguese captain's cabin, or Wilson's visit to the brothel, the author makes no attempt to spare the fastidious reader. Violent death, suicide and disease lurk around every corner. The veneer of respectability, fair play and Puritan morality is stripped away; and despite notable exceptions – Scobie's honesty, Ali's loyalty, Helen's disinterested declaration of love, the short-lived beauty of the port at sunset – lust and greed, betrayal and corruption, ugliness and decay, predominate. In its general impression, *The Heart of the Matter* may be said to be yet another illustration of 'Greeneland'.

Characters

Scobie

Most of the essential information about the hero is to be found in the Summaries. Let us recall the salient points.

As Wilson first sees him from the balcony of the Bedford Hotel—a squat grey-haired man (Bk. One, I, 1/1)—and as many subsequent incidents emphasise, Scobie appears as a rather ordinary, unromantic person. A dull middle-aged policeman in a small, unimportant colony, who had been passed over for promotion, he has no obvious faults: 'He didn't drink, he didn't fornicate, he didn't even lie' (Bk. Two, I, 1/1). At the start we learn that he has come to love the colony, the native people and his job, which he has reduced to the bare essentials. Gradually his exceptional character is revealed: he is 'honest and truthful'; scrupulously fair ('Scobie the Just' the Commissioner calls him); profoundly pessimistic (Bk. One, III, 1/1; Bk. Two, I, 1/3); weighed down by his feelings of responsibility and pity (Bk. Two, I, 1/3). His wife seems exasperated by his charity (Bk. Three, I, 2/2); Yusef is dumbfounded by his sense of honour (Bk. One, III, 1/1); even the mean-spirited Wilson says 'You are too damned honest to live' (Bk. Two, I, 1/1). A practising Catholic, he nevertheless questions the teaching of the Church after Pemberton's suicide (Bk. One, III, 1/1), or over his affair with Helen (Bk. Three, I, 1/1); and God's wisdom in letting the little girl survive drowning (Bk. Two, I, 1/4) or leaving him with 'a feeling of responsibility . . . like a sack of bricks' (Bk. Three, II, 2/1). In wishing always to bear the brunt he may be guilty of the sin of pride; but it is always others who come first. 'He never had any trust in mercy—except for other people' (Bk. Three, III, 1/3), says Father Rank at the end: this is truly Scobie's epitaph.

He is certainly not without defects. Capable of anger, as he shows when Louise is spoken of disparagingly at the Club, or when he is interrogated by the Colonial Secretary and Colonel Wright, he can indulge in petty revenge (by excluding Fraser from the inspection of the *Esperança* (Bk. One, I, 1/6) or in a certain cruelty (to Fellowes when he says 'Perhaps you've never lost anything of any importance'—Bk. Two, III, 2/1). Moreover he seems to lack sympathy and imagination in his relations with his wife (Bk. One, I, 1/4; Bk. One, I, 2/4) and even with Helen when she fails to understand his spiritual dilemma (Bk. Three, I, 3/1). His remark to Yusef 'I have a prose mind' (Bk. Three, I, 4/1) does not refer only to literature. Besides, though he is, as Wilson thinks, unused to practise deceit (Bk. Two, III, 1/2) he can, on his own admission, be 'corrupted by sentiment' (Bk. One, I, 2/3); and this is perhaps his chief weakness. He had always felt responsible for the happiness of those he loved (Bk. One, I, 1/3); and this theme runs right through the novel. His easily awakened pity and his persistent sense of responsibility lead to his own moral decline, to the unhappiness of the two women and finally to his suicide. Of course there are moments of happiness—on trek with Ali, carrying out routine duties, after his first visit to Helen—but basically he is doomed to unhappiness because he is seeking the impossible: 'happiness for others and peace and solitude for himself' (Bk. Two, III, 1/3). The two people who are closest to him —Louise and Helen—realise this perfectly well. Few readers would endorse the author's view expressed in the revised edition of the novel (1971) (p. XIV): 'The character of Scobie was intended to show that pity can be the expression of an almost monstrous pride.' For most, the hero's sense of duty, his profound goodness, his inability to be happy when those around him are unhappy, make him a deeply moving person, impossible to ignore or forget. Out of apparently unpromising material, Graham Greene has created a character who must surely be one of the outstanding achievements in modern fiction.

Louise

A middle-aged product of the English middle class, Scobie's wife appears unattractive, both physically and morally. Unlovely to look at, she is ageing badly (Bk. Three, II, 3/2), so that it is difficult to imagine her young and pretty. Her husband sees her as lacking in taste and tact (Bk. One, I, 1/4), losing her friends through condescension and snobbery, given to literary pretensions (Bk. One, III, 1/3). Moreover she is excessively pious, urging her husband to his religious duties (Bk. One, I, 1/3; Bk. Three, I, 1/1), emphasising her, or their, Catholicism (Bk. Three, I, 2/1; II, 1/2; III, 1/3), which contrasts sharply with her selfishness (Bk. One, I, 1/3), her insensitivity to Ali's death (Bk. Three, II, 1/2), her treachery in forcing Scobie to attend Communion when she knows what this implies. Even the re-insertion of the scene played between Mrs Scobie and Wilson at the beginning of Book One,

Part II, Chapter 2/1, designed, as the author tells us, 'to put Mrs Scobie's character in a more favourable light' (see Introduction to 1971 edition, p. XIV) does little to redress the balance in her favour.

On the other hand, we must remember that she has lost her only daughter; is unpopular and virtually friendless in the colony she has come to hate; is bitterly and understandably disappointed at her husband's failure to be promoted. Moreover she is not without good qualities, showing solicitude when Scobie leaves for Bamba (Bk. One, II, 2/2) or complains of a pain in the chest (Bk. Three, I, 1/2); shrewdness in judging Wilson (Bk. One, III, 1/3), and dignity in dealing with him; understanding in gauging her husband's character— 'Without me you'll have peace' she says (Bk. One, I, 2/4).

Perhaps Graham Greene loads the dice against her, letting us see her mainly through Scobie's eyes; mocking her love of modern poetry; linking her with the deplorable Wilson. At all events we breathe a sigh of relief when she departs towards the end of Book One and the atmosphere becomes more oppressive when she returns at the beginning of Book Three. In contradiction with her declared Christian faith, she is spiteful and unforgiving at the end. She is a vivid creation; but an unpleasing one.

Helen

The second woman in Scobie's life, Helen, first appears in Book Two when she is landed with the other survivors from the torpedoed ship (Bk. Two, I, 1/2). She is grasping a stamp-album and wearing a wedding-ring 'loose on the finger, as though a child had dressed up' (Bk. Two, I, 1/3). She is present a little later when Scobie reads to the schoolboy and the next we see of her is when the police officer glimpses a light from her Nissen hut during black-out. She is physically undistinguished (Bk. Two, I, 2/1); ill-educated, mistaking Virgil for Homer (Bk. Two, I, 2/1), mis-spelling common words (Bk. Two, III, 2/1); socially conventional (Bk. Two, III, 2/1). Despite the thirty years' gap in age and her obvious immaturity, she and Scobie become lovers at their second meeting. Quickly embittered by the strain of a clandestine love affair (Bk. Two, III, 1/1) Helen grows reproachful and jealous, reminding Scobie in a way of Louise, 'educated by love and secrecy' (Bk. Two, III, 1/1). Helen has no religious faith and finds it difficult to understand Scobie's scruples, though still loving him deeply. The only real love scene in the book takes place when they meet after Ali's death and Helen declares her feelings, with great tenderness and haunting lyricism (Bk. Three, II, 1/1). The end of the novel shows her ready for 'slutting with Bagster'; but longing for Scobie. Helen arouses our compassion by her youth and ignorance of the world, by her early widowhood and by her deep feeling for Scobie. In contrast with Louise she is capable, as her letter shows, of the love that puts the loved one first.

Wilson

Specially sent from London to investigate the diamond smuggling and to report on the activities of the British officials in the colony, Wilson becomes involved in Scobie's life, both in his capacity as a spy and because he falls in love with Scobie's wife. In the introduction to the revised edition of 1971, the author tells us that originally Wilson was to have been the hero of the novel; but that he 'obstinately refused to come alive' (p. XV). Through his actions as a spy he is an essential part of the intrigue; he quickly appears too undignified, too theatrical and too petty to win our sympathy, let alone our esteem. Right from the beginning he appears slightly absurd, with his unsuitable clothes, his lack of self-assurance and his determination to conceal his love of poetry from all but Louise. But any tendency we may have to pity him is quickly dispelled by his confrontations with Scobie, at Pende (Bk. Two, I, 1/5) and on the quay (Bk. Three, I, 4/1); by his attempts to make love to Louise; by his ludicrous behaviour in the brothel; by his nasty, prying mind. With his bad poetry, his blatant insincerity and his contemptible behaviour, he must be the most unattractive spy in modern fiction, perhaps too unattractive to be credible.

Yusef

With his large pasty face, huge thighs, hairy chest and glistening, oily skin, Yusef is hardly a prepossessing figure. His character—wily, untrustworthy, ingratiating and sentimental—does little to compensate for his repulsive appearance. Much cleverer than his Catholic fellow-countryman Tallit (whom he constantly double-crosses), he holds innumerable facts and figures in his head; is using the war to feather his own nest, by hoarding cotton and smuggling diamonds; and can worm his way out of any tricky situation. His astute use of gifts and spying servants has won him an exceptional place in the colony; and he does not baulk at blackmail, informing and murder. The overall impression then is sinister, that of a man who is the very symbol of corruption and the abuse of power. Moreover he must bear some responsibility for Scobie's downfall.

Nevertheless his genuine affection for the Deputy Commissioner, his sense of humour, his hunger for culture (illustrated for example by his interest in Shakespeare) and his nostalgia for goodness, show him to be something more than 'the dirty dog' Father Rank describes (Bk. One,

II, 1/2). Moreover Scobie himself is strongly drawn to him, saying on two occasions 'You aren't a bad chap, Yusef' (Bk. One, III, 1/1; Bk. Two, I, 2/4); and there is no doubt that he shows generosity over Pemberton's debts, concern over Scobie's illness at Bamba, and, towards the end, a real desire to protect the latter from exposure (Bk. Three, I, 4/1).

If his morals are not often those extolled in Western societies, he appears to lack the hypocrisy frequently found there, while his sentimental, expansive nature neatly offsets British reticence. Altogether he is a vivid, indeed unforgettable, creation, with his gross body and his complex character. Besides, his part in the story is of the first importance, since it is he who lends money to Scobie, he who blackmails Scobie and he who (apparently) engineers the death of Ali.

Ali

'Short and squat with the broad ugly pleasant face of a Temne' (Bk. One, I, 1/3), Ali has served Scobie for fifteen years when the story begins, rising from 'small boy' to steward. They have clearly become deeply attached to one another, as is shown by a number of incidents: Ali dressing Scobie's cut hand (Bk. One, I, 1/7); serving him with tea on the trek (Bk. One, III, 1/1); tending his fever and guarding his sick room at Bamba (Bk. One, III, 1/1). Remembering earlier journeys and seeing Ali's face reflected in the driver's mirror, Scobie feels a wave of affection (Bk. One, I, 1/1). Loyal and attentive, Ali has resisted all attempts by others to steal his services whenever Scobie is away on leave; he is the embodiment of fidelity and reliability. It is Ali who is always at hand, waking his master with early morning tea, awaiting a late return from the Fellowes dinner party (Bk. Two, III, 2/1). Scobie's first doubts of Ali reflect his own moral decline, his yielding to deceit and corruption. To the end, Ali maintains and demonstrates his honesty, answering Scobie's probing questions with 'I'm your boy' (Bk. Three, I, 3/1). In this his good faith is corroborated by Helen: 'Don't frighten him . . . . He's telling the truth', she says to Scobie, and later, 'You can trust him, anyway' (Bk. Three, I, 3/1).

Ali is only seen through Scobie's eyes; but clearly he is of the same kind in his honesty and industry, his loyalty and kindness. Ali's death is Scobie's greatest punishment, a strong factor in his decision to commit suicide. It is deeply moving too, given the person and the betrayal involved. It should also be remembered that Ali is the only native African presented in any detail (the other 'boys', odd policemen, Miss Wilberforce and the mammy in the brothel being only sketchily described).

Father Rank

Briefly sketched in as a person, Father Rank is mainly significant as a representative of the Catholic Church. Discounting his brief appearance when Louise and Wilson are sheltering in the disused station (Bk. One, I, 2/1), we see him seven times, twice when he is hearing Confession, twice when he is officiating at Communion and three times when he may be said to be meeting people on equal terms. At Scobie's first Confession he appears almost brisk and business-like: 'The penance I would give to a lot of people . . . is six months' leave. The climate gets you down' (Bk. Two, I, 2/5). On the second occasion, when Scobie confesses to adultery, he seems strangely unhelpful, depressingly orthodox (Bk. Three, I, 2/2). Perhaps his first appearance—at Tallit's dinner party—when he seems shallow, hearty and gossipy, should have prepared us for his failure to offer spiritual comfort. At Mass he is invested with the dignity of his office (Bk. Three, I, 1/2; 2/2), stressing the solemn nature, for Scobie, of the Communion Service. His earlier appeal to Scobie emphasises his limitations as a priest: 'I've never been any good to the living, Scobie' he says (Bk. Two, III, 1/2). He has probably guessed (or heard) about Scobie's affair with Helen before this visit. Ultimately his insignificance as a priest is redeemed by his charity, his dismissal of silly Catholic jargon, his faith in God's mercy, his belief in Scobie's goodness.

Minor characters

There are a number of minor characters in the novel, briefly sketched but often memorably portrayed: Harris, the cable censor, is a good foil to Wilson in his desire to help and inform, his yearnings to belong, to be happy. His eagerness to befriend Wilson; his cockroach-hunting; his attitude to his old school, show him to be at once shallow and pathetic. Robinson, the bank manager, moving from restless hypochondria to stoic acceptance of approaching death is a vivid creation. Fraser, with his popular song fresh from England, his shallow jests and spiteful remarks, is as insignificant as the oversexed Bagster, while the Commissioner, who sees through the hypocrisy and snobbery of so many British members of the colony, knows Scobie's true value and is irked by officialdom, and the overworked, friendless priest at Bamba, Father Clay, with his narrow orthodoxy, pious taste in literature and occasional hallucinations, present a more admirable side of the colony. Other figures who linger in the mind are Perrot, the D.C. at Pende, with his laboured irony and self-importance; Mrs Bowles, the missionary's wife, with her efficiency, puritanism and rather chilling sense of duty. The stupid Mrs Halifax and the condescending Mrs Carter, the sentimental Portuguese Captain and the unbending French officer, doctors, policemen, 'boys', torpedoed survivors, all serve to create the impression of a heterogeneous community, in which the dominant groups are the British officials and the native races. Each one plays a useful part in suggesting local colour or in strengthening the narrative.

Language and style

Thorough knowledge of some of the masters (Dickens, R.L. Stevenson, Henry James (1843–1916), Joseph Conrad), experience as a journalist on *The Times* and *The Spectator*, an innate feeling for words, all these taught Graham Greene to write clearly and vividly. *The Heart of the Matter*, written about halfway through his career as a novelist, is a good example of his mature style: lucid and elegant, yet simple and unobtrusive. Like all great writers, he uses simile and metaphor effectively (and indeed abundantly), as a few examples will show.

Similes

Of Wilson—'he wore his moustache *like* a club tie' (Bk. One, I, 1/1). Of Fraser's face—'blank *as* a school notice-board out of term' (Bk. One, I, 2/3). Of polite conversation 'The phrases went to and fro *like* shuttlecocks' (Bk. Two, III, 2/1). Of the murdered Ali—'The body lay coiled and unimportant *like* a broken watchspring' (Bk. Three, I, 4/1). Of God's voice reasoning with Scobie—'it spoke *like* a dealer in a market' (Bk. Three, II, 2/1).

Metaphors

Of Louise's ambition—'She would have steered agilely up the ladders and left the snakes alone' (Bk. One, I, 1/2). Of Scobie at confession, 'kneeling in the space of an upturned coffin' (Bk. Three, I, 2/2).

Students should make their own list of similes and metaphors, classifying them by subject. There are a great many and they are often memorable.

Varieties of English include Negro speech, whether in mispronunciation such as 'sah' or 'massa', in words used in a special way such as 'palaver' or 'humbug' (see Notes and glossary) or in the constant substitution of the present for the past; the peculiar semi-cultivated style employed by Yusef ('You give an evil name to a dog and the dog is finished' (Bk. One, III, 1/1) for 'Give a dog a bad name and hang him'); the immature public school slang of Wilson and Harris (Bk. Two, II, 1/1) and the more sophisticated jargon of the established members of the colony (jiggers, bow-wows, Froggies, chop—see Notes and glossary); the Scotch accent of the engineer and the studied English of the French officer (Bk. Two, I, 1/2). The handling of dialogue is masterly throughout, deftly adapted to speaker and situation, while the skill in *description and narration* is illustrated in many passages, for example, the snapshot in Scobie's office drawer (Bk. One, I, 1/2), the port at sunset (Bk. One, I, 1/4), the human wharf rats (Bk. One, I, 1/6), Scobie interviewed by the M.I.5 representative (Bk. Two, I, 2/2), the death of the child at Pende (Bk. Two, I, 1/3), Scobie with Helen when Bagster knocks at the door of the Nissen hut (Bk. Two, I, 3/1), Scobie in Yusef's office waiting for Ali (Bk. Three, II, 4/1) and so on.

The *interior monologue* (a fictional character's sequence of thought or feeling, revealed by extended monologue) is used to reveal Scobie's inner self, in particular his relationship with his wife (Bk. One, III, 1/2; Bk. Three, II, 3/2), and with Helen (Bk. Two, I, 3/1; Bk. Three, II, 3/2) and his struggles with his conscience (Bk. Two, III, 1/3; Bk. Three, I, 1/2, 2/2; Part II, 2/1, 3/2). The letters written by some of the characters (the Portuguese captain's to his daughter, Scobie's to his wife, Helen's to Scobie) also cast new light on the writers. Finally there are a host of *wise and penetrating reflexions* on life and death, love and happiness, pity and responsibility, on human behaviour generally, an extensive list of which would constitute a veritable anthology of aphorisms. While each reader will certainly have his own preferences, a brief selection may help to highlight this aspect of the novelist's art:

'Despair is the price one pays for setting oneself an impossible task' (Bk. One, I, 2/4), 'A policeman should be the most forgiving person in the world if he gets the facts right' (Bk. One, II, 2/2), 'It's never any good lying to oneself .... One sees through the lie too easily' (Bk. Three, I, 4/1), 'In human relations kindness and lies are worth a thousand truths' (Bk. One, I, 2/4). Over and over again such thought-provoking statements, applicable to so many human situations, are made with memorable clarity and force.

Humour and irony

The association of humour with Graham Greene is not obvious, since the overall impression of his work (novels, short stories, plays) is a serious, often a sombre one. The themes of the great novels do not suggest humour, while the 'entertainments' arouse excitement more often than laughter. Yet when one looks more closely, one finds many humorous touches, often introduced, as in the present novel, to relieve tension or, more simply, to provide a fuller picture of life. In *The Heart of the Matter*, the humour ranges from the purely farcical to the subtleties of understatement and comic behaviour. A few examples of different kinds of humour are listed below:

Farce

Brigstock's drunken talk at the Club (Bk. One, I, 1/4); Harris and Wilson cockroach-hunting (Bk. One, II, 1/3); Wilson stretched out with a bleeding nose before Louise (Bk. Three, I, 2/1).

Verbal humour

The Portuguese captain's mistake over the expression 'not quite cricket' (Bk. One, I, 2/2); Harris's parody of Belloc's poem (Bk. One, I, 1/1); the author's mockery of modern poetry ('Louise said, "A lovely poem about a pylon"'—Bk. One, I, 1/2); Scobie's frequent mockery of Yusef; and the latter's mixture of English (see above, p.42).

Humour of character

The feather-headed Mrs Halifax who reads the same novels over and over again without realising it (Bk. One, I, 1/4); Yusef on his relations with women (Bk. Three, I, 4/1); Harris in his new dwelling, *missing* the cockroaches (Bk. Two, II, 1/1); Scobie rebuking Fellowes for his disbelief in hell (Bk. Two, III, 2/1); Perrot's heavy humour about the authorities in the capital of the colony (Bk. Two, I, 1/1).

Understatement

Scobie reflecting on the Portuguese captain's heart (Bk. One, I, 2/2) or replying to Helen about the rain (Bk. Two, I, 2/1) or sizing up the mission collection of books (Bk. Two, I, 1/4).

Humorous scenes

Scobie reading to the boy in hospital and transforming a pious Victorian record into an exciting adventure tale (Bk. Two, I, 1/4); Scobie listening to Helen's school recollections (Bk. Two, I, 2/1); Wilson trapped in the brothel (Bk. Two, II, 1/4).

In general, the more sophisticated humour belongs to Scobie, the farcical scenes to Wilson; but there is a good deal of both kinds of humour throughout the novel and the comic parts are not limited to these two.

Irony

There are many examples of irony in *The Heart of the Matter*, as when Louise questions the validity of her husband's Catholicism (Bk. One, I, 1/3); when the Portuguese captain says 'If you had a daughter you'd understand' (Bk. One, I, 2/2); when Father Rank declaims Scobie's incorruptibility (Bk. One, II, 1/2); when Scobie confidently reflects about his relationship with Helen: 'They were friends who could never be anything else than friends' (Bk. Two, I, 2/1); when Harris naively refers to Wilson as 'The damned elusive Pimpernel' (Bk. Two, I, 2/3), i.e. a secret agent. But the most effective touches concern suicide— Scobie thinking, after Pemberton has taken his own life, 'this was an act he could never do' (Bk. One, III, 1/1); Dr Sykes asserting 'I don't think any of us are likely . . . ' (Bk. Two, III, 2/1); Wilson saying at the end 'I thought it was suicide' (Bk. Three, II, 1/1)—and Louise's incomplete knowledge of the facts (Bk. Three, I, 1/1, 3/2.)

Part 4

Hints for study

BEFORE STUDYING THE COMMENTARY or consulting the Notes and glossary sections, the novel should be read right through as a story, and any personal impressions of it recorded, such as the narrative and descriptive qualities (or defects); the creation of atmosphere and background; the characterisation; the literary gifts (or shortcomings). After this first reading, it might be well to attempt a short account of the book as if you were invited to do so for a literary review or magazine.

The next stage would be to establish the exact order of events, which may prove difficult because of the movement from one place to another, and the shift from main plot (Scobie's adventures) to sub-plot (Wilson's activities). How much time elapses between our first sight of the hero and his death, between the various subdivisions in the novel?

It is rewarding to consider the creation of background and atmosphere by listing precise details concerning climate and speech, food and clothes, fauna and flora, architecture and social life. With the setting firmly in mind, you may then pass on to a careful study of the characters, writing down a full appreciation of the major ones (Scobie, Wilson, Louise, Helen, Yusef, Ali) and brief notes on the secondary figures (priests, other members of the British colony, black servants, survivors of the torpedoed boat, ship's captain, French officer, and so on). It would be profitable to pinpoint the role of every character in the story. What is the precise function of each? This exercise is expecially valuable if we ask ourselves about the circumstances of the appearance of each character on the scene, and note what is said by, to, and about the person in question. Do the characters develop? Are they psychologically consistent? Are they credible? At this stage a useful cross-comparison might be made with the notes on the characters in the 'Commentary'.

The ground has now been cleared for a more general study of the novel. *The Heart of the Matter* may reasonably be examined successively from a religious, social, narrative and artistic point of view.

(*a*) Isolate the religious scenes in the story and the specific references to Catholic doctrine. Do you feel these are overdone or that they interfere with our response to the work? If they were eliminated, or reduced in scope, would the novel lose some of its power?

(*b*) Is the author unfair to the members of the British colony, caricaturing their vanity, snobbery, narrow-mindedness? Could the book be considered as a social satire? Does it unjustly neglect the positive achievements of the colonisers? Where do Graham Greene's sympathies appear to lie? Such queries may lead you to change your view of the novel.

(*c*) How do you judge *The Heart of the Matter* as a story? Is it gripping and exciting (see Model answer (1))? Is it well told (see Commentary—Language and style)? Is there a tendency to overstress the sordid and the seedy? If you think so, then a list of such scenes, or descriptive touches, should be drawn up.

In dealing with examination questions great attention should be paid to accuracy and relevance. Avoid general statements which you cannot support or illustrate by precise reference or quotation. Do not accept the judgements of the critics, however eminent, if these do not coincide with your own views and convictions. Present your findings and opinions sincerely and fearlessly. Any examiner worth his salt will appreciate honesty and freshness and reward it accordingly.

Proposed questions for detailed study

(1) Consider *The Heart of the Matter* as a thriller.
(2) Examine the novel as a picture of life in a British colony.
(3) 'Scobie's dilemma is both religious and psychological.' Discuss.
(4) Compare and contrast Louise and Helen.
(5) Compose brief portraits of *three* of the following: Yusef, Ali, Wilson, Harris, Robinson, the Commissioner, Father Rank, Fellowes.

Model answers

(1) Consider *The Heart of the Matter* as a thriller.

(*a*) *Definition of a thriller*
If we accept the dictionary definition of a thriller as 'a work of fiction or drama designed to hold the interest by the use of a high degree of action, intrigue, adventure and suspense', at first sight our novel does not easily fit into this category. Yet more careful study will show that all these elements are present in the work; and that the influence of the cinema and of detective fiction is considerable. It should also be recalled that from the beginning Graham Greene's

novels owe much to Robert Louis Stevenson and Joseph Conrad in both of whose work the *story* is pre-eminent, a point which is emphasised by certain of Greene's titles—*A Gun for Sale*, *The Confidential Agent*, *The Ministry of Fear*.

(*b*) *Action and adventure*

Despite the number of reflective passages and the frequent use of monologue, the narrative carries us briskly along. We move rapidly from the police station to Scobie's house, from there to the Club, to routine inspections, to visits outside the capital, to scenes in Helen's hut, Yusef's house, the Commissioner's office. We are on board ship several times, we accompany Scobie to Bamba, to Pende, to Yusef's office. Wilson confronts Scobie (and Louise), Scobie confronts Yusef and the Colonial Secretary, and is himself confronted by Helen and Louise and indeed, by God. Smuggling and spying, interrogation and love-making, murder, death and suicide are all part of the story. What is usually regarded as a psychological novel is in fact full of action and adventure.

(*c*) *Intrigue*

Wilson's spying activities—however clumsily carried out—form an essential part of the story, complicated as they are by his love for Louise and his jealousy of Scobie. By putting himself into Yusef's hands, Scobie becomes involved in the diamond-smuggling, and his clandestine love affair with Helen makes him increasingly vulnerable. All these threads of intrigue are cleverly intertwined: spying and wartime conditions, Scobie's need for money and his relations with Yusef, Louise's absence in South Africa and Helen's arrival from the torpedoed ship.

(*d*) *Suspense*

Above all, the novel approaches the classic thriller in its use of suspense. The reader has only to think of Scobie searching the Portuguese captain's cabin with the latter standing behind him (Bk. One, I, 2/2) or destroying the hidden letter just as Fraser approaches (Bk. One, I, 2/3); of the missing letter, written by Scobie to Helen; of the anguished night-long wait for Ali in Yusef's office; of Scobie at Confession and at Communion (will he confess all? will he take Communion?) or debating his projected suicide with God.

The Heart of the Matter can therefore be considered as a thriller from many angles. If we say that it is a gripping story we are in no way detracting from its value as a work of art, for here the psychological novel has been marvellously adapted to the framework of the thriller.

(2) Examine the novel as a picture of life in a British colony.

(a) Physical description

The novel is based on Graham Greene's own experience of life in Sierra Leone, when he was working there for the Foreign Office in 1942–3. In an introductory note, the author himself states: 'The geographical background of the story is drawn from that part of West Africa of which I have had personal experience.' As a result, the physical background of the story is vividly and accurately depicted. The oppressive climate, with its alternation of rains and relentless sun; the landscapes of swamps and rivers, low hills and laterite roads, 'bush villages of mud and thatch' (Bk. One, III, 1/1); the fauna and flora; the constant presence of rats and lizards, pye dogs and vultures, mosquitoes and cockroaches; the strange mixture of races—all combine to create an authentic picture, a view of the country through European, even English, eyes. In the capital, the massive Victorian buildings, Nissen huts and outlying bungalows help to set the scene. It is against this background that the course of events must be seen, and the actions of the characters judged. The setting and the atmosphere have a vital influence on the way people think and behave.

(b) The British presence

The British presence in the colony is pervasive. The structure of government with its network of administrative officials, law courts, police stations and prisons, provides the very fabric of the novel. As an instrument of British rule, Scobie is seen carrying out many duties: interrogating Miss Wilberforce (Bk. One, I, 1/2); conferring with the Commissioner; touring the unsavoury wharf at night; visiting Bamba after Pemberton's suicide; receiving the survivors at Pende; inspecting the Portuguese liner. Key figures in the country's professional, religious, economic and administrative life—bank managers, doctors and dentists, sanitary inspectors, priests and missionaries—bear witness to the ownership of the colony.

(c) The British colony

This ownership is stressed by the attempts of the British ruling class to maintain a British way of life (at least for themselves) and to safeguard British values. Thus the British abroad continue to drink gin and dress for dinner; congregate in a club that endeavours to preserve an exclusive character; gather at the beach to engage in idle gossip. Though much native food is consumed (but remember that a piece of Argentine beef is the chief attraction at Fellowes's dinner party – Bk. Two, III, 2/1), few concessions are made to native form of dress or local customs. The old school tie is a vital status symbol, the badge of respectability by which men are judged. Cut off from British standards and behaviour by distance, the British colony make every effort to keep the flag flying. Ill-equipped to deal with the hazards of such a hostile climate, they often fall victims to malaria or blackwater fever. Unable to comprehend the African mentality, they frequently suffer a nervous collapse or a loss of authority. Boredom during leisure time leads to pointless love affairs, excessive drinking or other vices. Even the priests show signs of strain.

(d) Greene's view of the colony

Graham Greene depicts his colonialists as uprooted, homesick, lonely, unhappy and ill at ease, yet clinging desperately to a British code, to the rules and regulations of their class. The result is usually xenophobia, often breakdown (Bk. One, I, 1/4). The characters are rarely endearing or intelligent, often snobbish, shallow and mean-spirited. Perhaps the picture may appear one-sided, with a notable lack of decent, kind, thoughtful people and by and large a disregard of the benefits of the colonial presence—better medical services, better roads and bridges, a sincere attempt to achieve justice. Yet if life in a British colony, as judged by *The Heart of the Matter*, seems sordid and unappealing, the portrait is carefully documented and vividly presented, an unforgettable account of a vanished way of life.

---

(4) Compare and contrast Louise and Helen

Despite outstanding differences in age, situation, behaviour and character, Louise and Helen have more in common than is immediately obvious. Both are conventional products of the English middle class, as constant references to their past, and their attitudes in the present, make clear. Both are lonely and unhappy; Louise because she has few friends, hates the colony and resents her husband's failure to gain promotion; Helen because she is a very young widow suddenly landed in a strange world where the company is uncongenial and the visits of the one person she loves clandestine and occasional. Both are physically unattractive (see under 'Characters') though Helen may be appealing, at times, by reason of her youth and helplessness. Both are intellectually outside the average run: Louise in her highbrow tastes (modern poetry, Virginia Woolf); Helen in her ignorance and immaturity—confusing Homer and Virgil, mis-spelling common words, holding on tenaciously to school memories, utterly failing to grasp Scobie's religious scruples. Both love Scobie and are genuinely concerned when his health seems in danger; yet both easily slip into reproaches, nagging and making scenes, thus adding to his burdens.

Nevertheless the differences between them are more striking. Louise is middle-aged and has been married for about fifteen years; Helen is widowed at the age of nineteen. However unpopular, Louise is protected and established in society, ambitious and worldly-wise (note her judgement of Wilson); Helen is too young and too alone to have such advantages. Louise has intellectual tastes and literary pretensions; Helen is startlingly ill-informed (her main success at school having been netball). Above all, Louise is a pious Catholic, with a strong tendency to stress her faith and its obligations, whereas Helen appears to be a typical English agnostic who dismisses Scobie's religious arguments as 'hooey' and easily accepts Bagster's vague reassurance about God at the end (Bk. Three, III, 1/2). Finally, while Louise emerges as a hard, selfish, unforgiving woman, Helen strikes us – for all her immaturity – as disinterested, tender and loving.

Ultimately *The Heart of the Matter* is the story of Scobie's unflagging resolve to make others happy even at the expense of his own principles and peace of mind. His relations with the two women are chiefly interesting in that both women illuminate his character and add to his dilemma. However different they may be, Louise and Helen are primarily used by the author to add to our knowledge of the hero, to show us the whole man. As a result, both the women are seen through Scobie's eyes, rarely viewed objectively nor allowed to develop independently. Helen is only seen once without Scobie, towards the end; Louise twice (on her hillside walk with Wilson, and with Father Rank, at the end). Considerable limitations are thus imposed on their psychological evolution and their validity as people. In spite of such restrictions they remain vividly in our minds.

---

(5) Compose brief portraits of *three* of the following: Yusef, Ali, Wilson, Harris, Robinson, The Commissioner, Father Rank, Fellowes.

(*a*) *Robinson*

We first meet Robinson in Book One, Part I, Chapter 2/1, when Scobie goes to the bank hoping to borrow money to send Louise to South Africa. The bank manager is briefly sketched: 'tall and hollow-chested and bitter because he hadn't been posted to Nigeria' (a more prestigious colony). With 'legs like stilts' and a restless manner, he sips iced water and walks to and fro incessantly in his little office to keep fit (three miles before lunch, he says!). Surrounded by medical books – 'A man's got to know what's wrong with him' – he is clearly an eccentric hypochondriac, if a kindly, even generous, man. As a stickler to rules, he refuses to allow Scobie an overdraft because of war regulations and dismisses the latter's tentative guarantees as inadequate security; but is willing to offer a personal loan.

On his second appearance in the novel (Bk. Three, I, 3/1), when Scobie visits him for the second time, Robinson is still 'stork-like', still drinking iced water; but the restless pacing up and down has given way to an attitude of calm repose at his desk. The medical books have been rejected in favour of medical advice, and Scobie is given the name of the doctor he subseqently consults. Scobie himself is too engrossed in reading about the symptoms of angina to catch Robinson's hints about the real state of his health, but learns a little later from the Commissioner that the bank manager has been given two years to live, which leads the hero to reflect: 'Human beings never cease to surprise: so it was the death sentence that had cured Robinson of his imaginary ailments, his medical books, his daily walk from wall to wall.'

Scobie's two visits to Robinson are vitally important in the story: the first marks his attempt to raise money for Louise's passage by straightforward means; the second shows his first steps towards suicide. Yet the bank manager is a very living portrait, in his own right: conscientious, odd and generous, early on; dignified, stoical and helpful towards the end. We would like to have seen more of this strange figure.

(b) The Commissioner

An 'old man of fifty-three', with twenty-two years' service, the Commissioner is the top security official in the colony. The absence of a name – he is always known as 'the Commissioner' – emphasises the significance of his function, perhaps also the impersonal nature of his actions. In four brief appearances we never get very close to him; but we learn to respect, even to like the man for his loyalty to Scobie.

(1) In Book One, Part I, Chapter 1/2, he officially announces his retirement to his second-in-command and conveys his disappointment that the latter is not to succeed him. His assessment of his chief assistant as 'Scobie the Just', his contempt for the malicious gossip of the people at the Secretariat about Scobie and his predecessors ('a lot of swine'), win our sympathy.

(2) The Commissioner next appears when Scobie is being questioned about the diamond smuggling by the Colonial Secretary and the M.I.5 representative, Colonel Wright (Bk. Two, I, 2/2). He says very little (too little perhaps?) but his uneasy embarrassment is conveyed by his constant whittling of his desk. His absence at Bamba

(for Pemberton's suicide) and at Pende (for the reception of the survivors) seems strange, although we know by then that Scobie does most of the work.

(3) His third appearance, when he invites his Deputy to dinner, renews our admiration. Faced with Wilson's spying activities, and Scobie's offer of resignation, he says 'You're the only officer I really trust' (Book Two, III, 1/3). Their spiritual kinship is memorably stated: 'Men can become twins with age: the past was their common womb.... They needed only a few words and a few gestures to convey their meaning.'

(4) Lastly the Commissioner informs Scobie that after all, he is to succeed to the top job (Bk. Three, I, 3/1). The news comes too late; but the accompanying words are genuine and warm-hearted. In this same brief scene Scobie learns the truth about Robinson.

The Commissioner remains a shadowy figure, almost justifying Wilson's judgement that he is 'too easy-going', conspicuous by his absence (as we have seen) on the big occasions, apparently unwilling to stick out his neck for his trusted Deputy; yet, all in all, a likeable, honourable man.

(c) Fellowes

We first meet Fellowes, the sanitary inspector, at the club (Bk. One, I, 1/4) where he is holding forth on the inadvisability of admitting people in trade to membership. Wilson, who is outwardly a U.A.C. clerk but in reality a government spy, has been brought along as a guest and wants to join the club. The author's description of Fellowes does nothing to endear him to us: 'the thin, damp ginger hair, the small prickly moustache, the goosegog eyes, the scarlet cheeks and the old Lancing tie'. Scobie's charitable attitude is supremely eloquent: 'Ever since Fellowes had snatched his house Scobie had done his best to like the man.... But sometimes he found it very hard to like Fellowes.' With his attachment to petty snobberies and insular taboos and rituals, Fellowes emerges as something of a satire of the English public school product abroad – shallow, provincial and unimaginative. Life in Africa and rubbing shoulders with people of different nationalities have done little to widen his horizons.

Fellowes then disappears from the novel until Book Two, Part III, Chapter 2/1, where he hosts a dinner party, at which the main excitement is the Argentine beef and at which Scobie and Helen meet, apparently as strangers. The conversation turns to suicide and Scobie tells Helen of his wife's imminent return. Apart from social patter and rakish jokes about Mrs Rolt (Helen), Fellowes strikes us mainly by his insensitivity about young Pemberton: 'A chap's got the right to take his own life, of course, but there's no need for fuss.'

There is so little to be said in favour of Fellowes that one wonders whether the author is not using him to vent his dislike for a certain kind of Englishman, and whether the caricature is not overdone. Nevertheless, as with Robinson, two short scenes suffice to create a living man – unpleasing in his person, limited in his outlook, uncharitable in his judgements.

Part 5

Suggestions for further reading

The text

The Heart of the Matter, Penguin Books, Harmondsworth, 1971. This is a reset reprint of the revised edition, published in 1971 by Heinemann, London, and The Bodley Head, London.

Other novels by Graham Greene

Brighton Rock (1938), *The Power and the Glory* (1940), *The End of the Affair* (1951) are of particular interest to the student of *The Heart of the Matter* because of their preoccupation with Catholic themes. Others, such as *Stamboul Train* (1932), *The Ministry of Fear* (1943), *Our Man in Havana* (1958), *The Comedians* (1966), and *The Human Factor* (1978) furnish fine examples of Graham Greene's narrative and descriptive gifts, his skill in conveying atmosphere and creating character.

Criticism

ALLEN, WALTER: 'The novels of Graham Greene', in *Penguin New Writing*, XVIII, pp. 148-60, Penguin Books, Harmondsworth, 1943.

ALLOTT, KENNETH AND FARRIS, MYRIAM: *The Art of Graham Greene*, Hamish Hamilton, London, 1963.

FORD, BORIS (ED.): *The Pelican Guide to English Litrature*, vol. 7, *The Modern Age*, Penguin Books, Harmondsworth, 1961.

MESNET, MARIE-BÉATRICE: *Graham Greene and The Heart of the Matter*, Cresset Press, London, 1954.

O'DONNELL, DONAT: *Maria Cross*, Chatto and Windus, London, 1953.

PANGE, VICTOR DE: *Graham Greene*, Editions Universitaires, Paris, 1953.

PRYCE-JONES, DAVID: *Graham Greene*, Oliver and Boyd, Edinburgh and London, 1963.

The author of these notes

MARK MORTIMER is a graduate of Dublin University. He has been teaching English language and literature at the British Institute in Paris since 1947, and is now senior lecturer there. He also teaches at the Institut d'Etudes Politiques (where he created a seminar on Ireland in 1969) and at the Ecole Nationale d'Administration. In 1976–9 he was 'maître de conférences associé' at the University of Lille.

He has published articles and reviews on Anglo-Irish literature in learned journals in France and Ireland, and has broadcast and lectured extensively in this field. He is the author of the York Notes on J.M. Synge's *The Playboy of the Western World*, and is at present working on a full-length critical review of J.M. Synge.

The first 250 titles

The first ten titles

YORK HANDBOOKS form a companion series to York Notes and are designed to meet the wider needs of students of English and related fields. Each volume is a compact study of a given subject area, written by an authority with experience in communicating the essential ideas to students of all levels.

AN INTRODUCTORY GUIDE TO ENGLISH LITERATURE
by MARTIN STEPHEN

PREPARING FOR EXAMINATIONS IN ENGLISH LITERATURE
by NEIL McEWAN

AN INTRODUCTION TO LITERARY CRITICISM
by RICHARD DUTTON

THE ENGLISH NOVEL
by IAN MILLIGAN

ENGLISH POETRY
by CLIVE T. PROBYN

STUDYING CHAUCER
by ELISABETH BREWER

STUDYING SHAKESPEARE
by MARTIN STEPHEN *and* PHILIP FRANKS

ENGLISH USAGE
by COLIN G. HEY

A DICTIONARY OF LITERARY TERMS
by MARTIN GRAY

READING THE SCREEN
An Introduction to Film Studies
by JOHN IZOD